Supporting Spelling

FOR AGES 11–12

Contents

Introduction

The *Supporting Spelling* series is aimed at all those who work with students who have been identified as needing 'additional' or 'different' literacy support. It can be used by anyone working with students who fall into this category, whether you are a teacher, classroom assistant or parent.

Typically, the eleven to twelve year-old students, for whom the book is intended, will be working at the levels expected of primary aged children or they may simply need extra help in tackling the level of work appropriate for Year 7. Their difficulties may be short-term, and overcome with extra practice and support on a one-to-one or small group basis, or they may be long-term, where such support enables them to make progress but at a level behind their peer group.

The activities in this book provide exactly what these students need – plenty of repetition and practice of spelling skills, based on close observation of words together with listening to the sounds within words. The students are encouraged to say the words and to listen to both the syllables and the phonemes from which the words are formed. Some students reach a level of maturity at the early secondary school stage where they can apply a 'retrospective phonics' approach to words, understanding the links between sounds and graphemes possibly for the first time. Within this book we provide an approach that is:

Systematic
Multi-sensory
Based on Speaking and Listening
Linked closely to reading skills

This book is organised into double page spreads. Each spread consists of a page of teachers' notes introducing specific words followed by a worksheet containing activities centred around these words. All the activities can be used on their own or alongside other literacy schemes that are already established within the school. The activities are simple and self-explanatory and the instruction text is kept to a minimum to make the pages easy to use for adults and less daunting for students to follow. Suggestions for additional activities are supplied if appropriate.

The words featured in this book are drawn from:

 (i)   the high and medium frequency words recommended for primary aged students;
 (ii) vocabulary suited for students at the early part of secondary school;
 (iii) lists of words that contain particular prefixes, suffixes, inflections and letter strings recommended for students at the early part of secondary school.

Students generally achieve the greatest success in an atmosphere of support and encouragement. Praise from a caring adult can be the best reward for the students' efforts. The worksheets and activities in this book will provide many opportunities for students to enjoy these successes. The development of a positive attitude and the resulting increase in self-esteem will help them with all of their schoolwork.

Record and Review

Name: _____ Date of birth: _____

Teacher: _____ Class: _____

Support Assistant: _____

Code of Practice stage: _____ Date targets set: _____

Target

1 _____

2 _____

3 _____

4 _____

Review

Target

1 _____

_____

_____ Target achieved? ☐ Date _____

2 _____

_____

_____ Target achieved? ☐ Date _____

3 _____

_____

_____ Target achieved? ☐ Date _____

4 _____

_____

_____ Target achieved? ☐ Date _____

Definitions and explanations of terms

Many documents use terminology that is unfamiliar to non-specialists and some definitions are listed below. Please note that some publications will give slightly different definitions.

Antonym
An antonym is a word that is opposite in meaning to another word, eg 'hot' and 'cold'. An antonym prefix is a prefix that creates a word that is opposite in meaning to another: e.g. 'un' added to 'necessary' creates 'unnecessary'.

Homonym
A homonym is a word having the same sound or spelling as another but which has a different meaning e.g. the word 'bow' can be the front of a boat or it can be the act of bending forward when an audience is applauding. But the word 'bow' with a different sound, as in a ribbon tied in a bow, is still a homonym.

Homophone
A homophone is a word having the same sound as another word but with different meaning or spelling e.g. the words 'bear' and 'bare' are homophones.

Inflection
An inflection is a suffix that is used to change a word to show tense, gender, number, etc. e.g. 'ed' is an inflection that can be added to a word to change its tense: 'climb' – 'climbed'.

Prefix
A prefix can be placed at the beginning of an existing word to change its meaning e.g. 'dis' can be placed at the beginning of 'advantage'.

Suffix
A suffix can be placed at the end of an existing word to change its meaning e.g. 'al' can be added to the end of 'music'.
(Note, out of interest, that the 'ic' in 'music' is itself a suffix that was incorporated into the Greek word mousike, meaning 'of the Muses'. Thus words such as epic, critic and music can all be said to have the suffix 'ic' although the suffix has not been added to a modern word.)

Synonym
A synonym is a word that means the same or nearly the same as another word e.g. 'jump' and 'leap'.

The following definitions and explanations all relate to terminology used in relation to phonics.

Phoneme	A phoneme is a unit of sound and can be represented by:
	one letter, e.g. **b** as in **b**at two letters, e.g. **ee** as in sw**ee**t three letters, e.g. **ear** as in n**ear**
	Note that a phoneme (a sound) can be represented in several ways e.g. the sound /ee/ can be represented by:
	ee as in f**ee**t **ei** as in c**ei**ling **ie** as in ch**ie**f **ea** as in n**ea**t **i** as in sk**i** **e_e** as in P**ete**
Vowel phoneme	A vowel phoneme makes an open sound and always contains at least one vowel – you usually have to open your mouth to say it. Examples of vowel phonemes are:
	/a/ as in b**a**t /ie/ as in cr**ie**s /oo/ as in b**oo**k /ur/ as in t**ur**n /ow/ as in t**ow**n
Consonant phoneme	A consonant phoneme always contains at least one consonant and usually involves closing the mouth, or 'biting' the lower lip, or touching the roof of the mouth with the tongue. (There are exceptions, e.g. /h/). Examples of consonants phonemes are:
	/b/ as in **b**at /f/ as in **ph**otograph /th/ as in **th**ey /ng/ as in si**ng**
Grapheme	A grapheme is a letter or pair of letters or group of letters representing a single sound e.g. **ee**, **ei**, **ie**, **ea**, **i** and **e_e** are all graphemes representing the sound /ee/.
Grapheme/phoneme correspondence	The relationship between letters and the sounds that they represent.

Digraph	A digraph consists of two letters representing a single sound. So, for example, the grapheme **ch** is a consonant digraph because it is made up of two consonants. The grapheme **ee** is a vowel digraph, but **ow** is also a vowel digraph, although it contains a consonant, because it makes an open sound like a vowel does.
Split digraph	A split digraph consists of two vowels separated by a consonant to make one phoneme e.g.

                  e_e as in Pete
                  i_e as in mine
                  a_e as in came

Trigraph	A trigraph is a group of three letters representing a single sound. The vowel phonemes /air/ and /ear/ are trigraphs.
Cluster	A cluster consists of two or more letters making more than one sound e.g.

        t   **h**   **r**   are three letters that can make the cluster **thr**, which consists of the phonemes /th/ and /r/.

Blending	Blending is the process of combining different sounds (phonemes) to be able to say a particular word or to make up part of a word e.g.

        /sh/   /i/   /p/   can be blended to make the word ship.

        /th/   /r/   are blended to make the cluster **thr**. Sometimes a cluster like this will be called a blend.

Segmenting	Segmenting is the process of splitting a word into its different phonemes to be able to spell the word e.g. **ship** can be segmented into the three phonemes /sh/ /i/ /p/.
vc	vowel/consonant, e.g. the word *it*
cv	consonant/vowel, e.g. the word *be*
cvc	consonant/vowel/consonant, e.g. the word *cat*
ccvc	consonant/consonant/vowel/consonant, e.g. the word *shop*
cvcc	consonant/vowel/consonant/consonant, e.g. the word *fast*

An introduction to phonemes

Language can be analysed by considering the separate sounds that combine to make up spoken words. These sounds are called phonemes and the English language has more than forty of them. It is possible to concentrate on forty-two main phonemes but here we list forty-four phonemes including those that are commonly used only in some regions of the country.

It is helpful to look at each phoneme then at some sample words that demonstrate how the phoneme is represented by different graphemes, as shown in the list below. Try reading each word out loud to spot the phoneme in each one. For the simple vowel sounds the graphemes are shown in bold text.

Vowel phonemes	Sample words
/a/	b**a**t
/e/	l**e**g, g**ue**ss, h**ea**d, s**ai**d, s**ay**s
/i/	b**i**g, plant**e**d, b**u**sy, cr**y**stal, d**e**cide, **e**xact, g**ui**lt, r**e**peat
/o/	d**o**g, **ho**nest, w**a**s, qu**a**rrel, tr**ou**gh, v**au**lt, **ya**cht (the ch is silent)
/u/	b**u**g, l**o**ve, bl**oo**d, s**o**me, c**o**mfort, r**ou**gh, **you**ng
/ae/	rain, day, game, navy, weigh, they, great, rein
/ee/	been, team, field, these, he, key, litre, quay, suite
/ie/	pie, high, sign, my, bite, child, guide, guy, haiku
/oe/	boat, goes, crow, cone, gold, sew, shoulder
/ue/	soon, do, July, blue, chew, June, bruise, shoe, you, move, through
/oo/	book, put
/ar/	barn, bath (regional), laugh (regional), baa, half, clerk, heart, guard
/ur/	Thursday, girl, her, learn, word
/or/	born, door, warm, all, draw, cause, talk, aboard, abroad, before, four, bought, taught
/ow/	brown, found, plough
/oi/	join, toy, buoy
/air/	chair, pear, care, where, their, prayer
/ear/	near, cheer, here, weird, pier

Try saying this vowel phoneme:

/er/	fast**er**, g**a**zump, curr**a**nt, wooll**e**n, circ**us**
	Not to be confused with the phoneme /ur/, this phoneme is very similar to /u/ but is slightly different in some regions.

Consonant phonemes	Sample words
/b/	bag, rub
/d/	dad, could
/f/	off, calf, fast, graph, tough
/g/	ghost, girl, bag
/h/	here, who
/j/	bridge, giraffe, huge, jet
/k/	kite, antique, cat, look, quiet, choir, sock, six (note that the sound made by the letter x is a blend of the phonemes /k/ and /s/)
/l/	leg, crawl, full
/m/	mug, climb, autumn, sum
/n/	now, gnash, knight, sign, fun
/p/	peg, tap
/r/	run, wrote
/s/	cinema, goose, listen, psalm, scene, see, sword, yes, less
/t/	ten, sit, receipt
/v/	vest, love
/w/	wet
/wh/	when (regional)
/y/	yes
/z/	choose, was, zoo
/th/	the, with
/th/	thank, path
/ch/	cheer, such, match
/sh/	shop, rush, session, chute, station
/zh/	usual
/ng/	thing, think

For some phonemes you may dispute some of the examples that we have listed. This may be due to regional variations in pronunciation. Disputing the sounds is a positive step as it ensures that you are analysing them!

It is certainly not necessary to teach the students all of the graphemes for each phoneme but to be ready and aware when they suggest words to you to represent a particular sound. They are not wrong with their suggestions and should be praised for recognising the phoneme. You can then show them how the words that they have suggested are written but that normally the particular sound is represented by a specific grapheme.

Words from the school timetable

1 Focus on words

- Photocopy this page and the accompanying student worksheet. Discuss the focus words at the bottom of this page with the students. (You may decide to change one or two to reflect the timetable used in your school.) Ask the students to write the words in the blank grid on their worksheet. You could dictate the words or, if appropriate, students could copy them from the set below.

- The completed grid on the worksheet, or the one below, could be laminated as a pocket reference card that students could refer to later.

- To analyse the words further, and if appropriate for your students, you could complete the following activities.

Segmenting the words into their phonemes

This is not an easy activity but the process encourages students to listen closely to the sounds that constitute the words. Explain to the students that they are going to segment some of the words into their separate sounds. Demonstrate this with the word *art* by drawing lines between the graphemes that represent the phonemes i.e. /ar/t/. Now look at *English*: /E/ng/l/i/sh/ and *religious*: /r/e/l/i/g/iou/s/. Ask the students to try with *music*, *science* and *Spanish*. They may come up with different answers from each other but the important part of the activity is the process of hearing the separate sounds and observing how they are represented by graphemes. Some words are particularly difficult to analyse in this way but this helps to draw attention to their particular letter strings. In the word *education* the students might find it difficult to decide how to segment the phonemes in **tion**. Through this they can learn that the letter string **tion** can be broken down into the phonemes /sh/u/n/.

Splitting the words into their syllables (syllabification)

For most students syllabification is much easier than segmenting. Explain that they are now going to split the words into 'chunks' of sound and give the example of *music*: \mu\sic\. Can the students hear how the word can be split into two syllables? Now look at *citizenship*: \ci\ti\zen\ship\ which has four syllables. Point out that each syllable normally contains at least one vowel.

2 Words in context

- When the students are ready ask them to complete the second activity on the worksheet in one of two ways. They can either attempt to read the sentences themselves and write the missing words or they can listen to you dictating the sentences and write the missing words as you dictate them.

- As an extension activity, have a blank timetable ready to discuss with the students. They could use this to try to show their own timetable as accurately as possible or they could be more creative e.g. they could design their ideal timetable according to set criteria such as: there must be at least one foreign language and all the other subjects must appear at least once.

Art	Music	Assembly	History
Geography	Science	Maths	Design Technology
Information and communication	Citizenship	English	Physical Education
French	German	Spanish	Religious Education

Words from the school timetable

Name _____

1 Write the focus words in the spaces on this grid.

2 Complete the following sentences.

a) The study of the past is called _____.

b) _____ is the language spoken in France.

c) You might read poems in an _____ lesson.

d) In _____ you often use an atlas when learning about other parts of the world.

e) In a _____ lesson you could play instruments.

f) The study of numbers and shapes is called _____.

g) Biology, Physics and Chemistry are all branches of _____.

h) Learning about beliefs such as Hinduism and Buddhism is called

_____   _____.

Which words from the school timetable grid were not included in the sentences?

_____   _____

_____   _____

_____   _____

Opposites 1

1 Focus on words

- Photocopy this page and the accompanying student worksheet. Discuss the focus words at the bottom of the page with the students. Ask them to write the words in the blank grid on their worksheet. You could dictate the words or, if appropriate, students could copy them from the set below.

- The completed grid on the worksheet, or the one below, could be laminated as a pocket reference card that students could refer to later.

- To analyse the words further, and if appropriate for your students, you could complete the following activities.

Segmenting the words into their phonemes

Explain to the students that they are going to segment some of the words into their separate sounds. Demonstrate with the word *below* by drawing lines between the graphemes that represent the separate phonemes i.e. /b/e/l/ow/. Now look at *answered*: /a/n/s/were/d/. This is a tricky word to deal with but encourage the students to say the word repeatedly, recognising the fact that the grapheme *were* is representing the phoneme /er/. Ask the students to try with *better* and *daughter*. They may come up with different answers from each other but the important part of the activity is the process of hearing the separate sounds and observing how they are represented by graphemes.

Splitting the words into their syllables (syllabification)

For most students syllabification is much easier than segmenting. Explain that they are now going to split the words into 'chunks' of sound and give the example of *adult*: \ad\ult\. Can the students hear how the word can be split into two syllables? Now look at *follow* and ask the students to compare it to *following*. Discuss some single syllable words with the students e.g. *took, can't*, etc. Point out that each syllable normally contains at least one vowel.

2 Words in context

- When the students are ready ask them to complete the second activity on the worksheet. The activity is in effect a comprehension task on the meanings of the words but also provides an excellent opportunity for spelling practice.

below	answered	better	mother
follow	never	baby	after
began	neither	brother	took
can't	adults	coming	didn't
different	doesn't	don't	first

Opposites 1

Name _____

1 Write the focus words in the spaces on this grid.

For each of the words below find a word that means the opposite, or nearly the opposite, from the words that you have written in the grid.

going _____   finished _____

lead _____   brought _____

before _____   does _____

last _____   always _____

asked _____   can _____

sister _____   worse _____

children _____   do _____

above _____   both _____

same _____   did _____

father _____   adult _____

2 Write a sentence using as many of the words above as you can. How crazy can you make your sentence?

_____

_____

_____

Opposites 2

1 Focus on words

- Photocopy this page and the accompanying student worksheet. Discuss the focus words at the bottom of this page with the students. Ask them to write the words in the blank grid on their worksheet. You could dictate the words or, if appropriate, students could copy them from the set below.

- The completed grid on the worksheet, or the one below, could be laminated as a pocket reference card that students could refer to later.

- Discuss some of the words in more detail e.g. point out that the letter **i** comes before the **e** in *friends*. You may like to introduce the tip 'i before e except after c' but note that there are exceptions, such as the word *their*. The words *light, high* and *right* all include the letter string **igh**.

- To analyse the words further, and if appropriate for your students, you could complete the following activities.

  Segmenting the words into their phonemes
  Explain to the students that they are going to segment some of the words into their separate sounds. Demonstrate this with the word *found* by drawing lines between the graphemes that represent the separate phonemes i.e. /f/ou/n/d/. Now look at *afternoon*: /a/f/t/er/n/oo/n/. Students may come up with different answers from each other but the important part of the activity is the process of hearing the separate sounds and observing how they are represented by graphemes.

  Splitting the words into their syllables (syllabification)
  For most students syllabification is much easier than segmenting. Explain that they are now going to split the words into 'chunks' of sound and give the example of *inside*: \in\side\. Can the students hear that the word can be split into two syllables? Now look at *important* and ask the students to compare it to *unimportant*. Point out that each syllable normally contains at least one vowel.

2 Words in context

- When the students are ready ask them to complete the second activity on the worksheet. The activity is in effect a comprehension task on the meanings of the words but also provides an excellent opportunity for spelling practice.

found	friends	goes	half
head	high	important	inside
lady	leave	light	morning
daughter	near	often	open
shut	right	small	happy

Opposites 2

Name _____

1 Write the focus words in the spaces on this grid.

For each of the words below find a word that means the opposite, or nearly the opposite, from the words you have written on the grid.

afternoon _____   big _____

stays _____   gentleman _____

open _____   low _____

unimportant _____   enemies _____

stay _____   closed _____

unhappy _____   far _____

tail _____   heavy _____

seldom _____   left _____

lost _____   whole _____

outside _____   son _____

2 Write a sentence using as many of the words above as you can. How crazy can you make your sentence?

_____

_____

_____

_____

Opposites 3

1 Focus on words

● Photocopy this page and the accompanying student worksheet. Discuss the focus words at the bottom of this page with the students. Ask them to write the words in the blank grid on their worksheet. You could dictate the words or, if appropriate, students could copy them from the set below.

● The completed grid on the worksheet, or the one below, could be laminated as a pocket reference card that students could refer to later.

● Discuss some of the words in more detail e.g. the word *sometimes* is a compound word, made from combining the words *some* and *times.* Encourage the students to notice that the two words are unchanged when combined in the compound word as students frequently miss the letter **e** from 'some'.

● To analyse the words further, and if appropriate for your students, you may like to complete the following activities.

Segmenting the words into their phonemes
Explain to the students that they are going to segment some of the words into their separate sounds. Demonstrate this with the word *started* by drawing lines between the graphemes that represent the phonemes i.e. /s/t/ar/t/e/d/. Ask the students to try some of the other words. They may come up with different answers from each other but the important part of the activity is the process of hearing the separate sounds and observing how they are represented by graphemes.

Splitting the words into their syllables (syllabification)
For most students syllabification is much easier than segmenting. Explain that they are now going to split the words into 'chunks' of sound and give the example of *together.* \to\ge\ther\ Can the students hear that the word can be split into three syllables? Ask them to try splitting some of the other words into syllables. Point out that each syllable normally contains at least one vowel.

2 Words in context

● When the students are ready, ask them to complete the second activity on the worksheet. The activity is in effect a comprehension task on the meanings of the words but also provides an excellent opportunity for spelling practice.

sometimes	started	still	suddenly
sure	together	under	walk
white	whole	woke	work
young	with	east	upstairs
beginning	present	night	north

Opposites 3

Name _____

1 Write the focus words in the spaces on this grid.

For each of the words below find a word that means the opposite, or nearly the opposite, to the words that you have written in the grid.

without _____   never _____

over _____   downstairs _____

past _____   unsure _____

stopped _____   day _____

play _____   moving _____

gradually _____   part _____

slept _____   old _____

west _____   apart _____

south _____   run _____

black _____   end _____

2 Write a sentence using as many of the words above as you can. How crazy can you make your sentence?

_____

_____

_____

_____

Day vocabulary

1 Focus on words

● Photocopy this page and the accompanying student worksheet. Discuss the focus words at the bottom of this page with the students. Ask them to write the words in the blank grid on their worksheet. You could dictate the words or, if appropriate, students could copy them from the set below.

● The completed grid on the worksheet, or the one below, could be laminated as a pocket reference card that students could refer to later.

● Discuss some of the words in more detail, e.g. the word *afternoon* is a compound word made from a combination of the words *after* and *noon*. Can the students spot another compound word in this list?

● To analyse the words further, and if appropriate for your students, you could complete the following activities.

Segmenting the words into their phonemes

Explain to the students that they are going to segment some of the words into their separate sounds. Demonstrate this with the word *Thursday* by drawing lines between the graphemes that represent the separate phonemes i.e. /Th/ur/s/d/ay/. The students may already have looked at the word *afternoon* as an example word on Worksheet 3 and you could now ask them to segment it themselves. They may come up with different answers from each other but the important part of the activity is the process of hearing the separate sounds and observing how they are represented by graphemes.

Splitting the words into their syllables (syllabification)

For most students syllabification is much easier than segmenting. Explain that they are now going to split the words into 'chunks' of sound and give the example of *today*: \to\day\. Can the students hear how the word can be split into two syllables? Now look at *Wednesday*. Ask the students to say it carefully. Can they work out which letters are silent?

2 Words in context

● When the students are ready ask them to complete the second activity on the worksheet in one of two ways. They can either attempt to read the sentences themselves and write the missing words or they can listen to you dictating the sentences and write the missing words as you dictate them.

Monday	Tuesday	Wednesday	Thursday
Friday	Saturday	Sunday	holiday
daily	birthday	morning	afternoon
evening	night	today	tomorrow
yesterday	during	every	between

Day vocabulary

Name _____

1 Write the focus words in the spaces on this grid.

2 Complete the following sentences:

My favourite day of the week is _____ because _____

_____

_____ .

The day I like least is _____ because _____

_____

_____ .

Today is _____ and _____ it will be

_____ .

Yesterday was _____ and the day before _____

was _____ .

My _____ is in _____ .

Every _____ I watch television before I go to bed.

I am supposed to get up early _____ _____ .

Adding ing

1 Focus on words

- Photocopy this page and the accompanying student worksheet. Discuss the focus words at the bottom of this page with the students. Ask them to write the words in the blank grid on their worksheet. You could dictate the words or, if appropriate, students could copy them from the set below.

- The completed grid on the worksheet, or the one below, could be laminated as a pocket reference card that students could refer to later.

- To analyse the words further, and if appropriate for your students, you could complete the following activities.

Segmenting the words into their phonemes

Explain to the students that they are going to segment some of the words into their separate sounds. Demonstrate this with the word *swimming* by drawing lines between the graphemes that represent the phonemes i.e. /s/w/i/mm/i/ng/. Ask the students to try with *answering*: /a/n/s/wer/i/ng/. (Note that this word contains a silent letter **w**, sometimes called an unsounded letter). They may come up with different answers from each other but the important part of the activity is the process of hearing the separate sounds and observing how they are represented by graphemes.

Splitting the words into their syllables (syllabification)

For most students syllabification is much easier than segmenting. Explain that they are now going to split the words into 'chunks' of sound and give the example of *following*: \fol\low\ing\. Can the students hear how the word can be split into three syllables? Point out that each syllable normally contains at least one vowel.

2 Using the 'ing' rules

- When the students are ready, ask them to look at the second activity on the worksheet. Discuss the 'rules' with the students, ensuring that they understand how each rule works, then help them to apply the rules to the activity.

swimming	thinking	trying	turning
following	walking	talking	watching
jumping	leaving	opening	beginning
owning	rounding	asking	answering
being	changing	coming	gardening

Adding ing

Name _____

1 Write the focus words in the spaces on this grid.

2 Rules about adding **ing**

- When a word ends in two consonants, just add **ing**
  e.g. think ⟶ thinking

- When a word ends in a vowel then a consonant, you usually double the consonant then add **ing**
  e.g. swim ⟶ swimming   begin ⟶ beginning

- But look at these:
  open ⟶ opening   garden ⟶ gardening   follow ⟶ following

- When a word ends with a consonant then **e**, take the **e** off then add **ing**
  e.g. change ⟶ changing

Use the rules to add **ing** to the words below. The first one has been done for you.

stop   _stopping_   float   _____

shop   _____   win   _____

come   _____   bring   _____

phone   _____   thank   _____

sing   _____   wash   _____

sink   _____   spot   _____

drip   _____   wear   _____

Words ending in **ed**

1 Focus on words

● Photocopy this page and the accompanying student worksheet. Discuss the focus words at the bottom of this page with the students. Ask them to write the words in the blank grid on their worksheet. You could dictate the words or, if appropriate, students could copy them from the set below.

● The completed grid on the worksheet, or the one below, could be laminated as a pocket reference card that students could refer to later.

● To analyse the words further, and if appropriate for your students, you could complete the following activities.

Segmenting the words into their phonemes
Explain to the students that they are going to segment some of the words into their separate sounds. Demonstrate this with the word *found* by drawing lines between the graphemes that represent the separate phonemes: /f/ou/nd/. Now look at *remembered*: /r/e/m/e/m/b/er/d/. They may come up with different answers from each other but the important part of the activity is the process of hearing the separate sounds and observing how they are represented by graphemes. *Remembered* is a very useful word to consider as so many students make mistakes with it.

Splitting the words into their syllables (syllabification)
For most students syllabification is much easier than segmenting. Explain that they are now going to split the words into 'chunks' of sound and give the example of *remembered*: \re\mem\bered\. Can the students hear that the word can be split into three syllables? Now look at *remember* and ask the students to compare it to *remembered*. Both words have three syllables but with *remembered*, **ed** has been added to create the past tense.

2 Using the 'ed' rules

● When the students are ready ask them to complete the second activity on the worksheet. Encourage them to notice that the rules are the same as for adding **ing**.

asked	changed	followed	headed
jumped	numbered	opened	owned
papered	placed	showed	started
stopped	turned	used	walked
watched	worded	worked	remembered

Words ending in ed

1 Write the focus words in the spaces on this grid.

2 Rules for adding **ed**

- When a word ends in two consonants, just add **ed** e.g. ask ⟶ asked

- When a word ends in a vowel then a consonant, you usually double the consonant then add **ed** e.g. stop ⟶ stopped

- But now look at these: open ⟶ opened   paper ⟶ papered
  follow ⟶ followed   remember ⟶ remembered

- When a word ends with a consonant then **e**, take the **e** off then add **ed** e.g. change ⟶ changed   place ⟶ placed

Use the rules to add **ed** to the words below. The first one has been done for you.

stop	_stopped_	drip	_____	wash	_____
shop	_____	float	_____	spot	_____
phone	_____	thank	_____	time	_____

The words ending with **ed** are all in the past tense

e.g. I remember your name.
   I remembered your name but now I have forgotten it!

For some words we do not add **ed** to make the past tense.

Match the present tense words to the past tense words. The first one has been done for you.

Present tense	Past tense
sing	won
sink	wore
win	heard
bring	sang
wear	began
begin	brought
hear	sank

Words ending in **al**

1 Focus on words

- Photocopy this page and the accompanying student worksheet. Discuss the focus words at the bottom of this page with the students. Ask them to write the words in the blank grid on their worksheet. You could dictate the words or, if appropriate, students could copy them from the set below.

- The completed grid on the worksheet, or the one below, could be laminated as a pocket reference card that students could refer to later.

- Discuss the idea of suffixes with the students. Explain that a suffix is a word ending that can be added to a word to change its meaning. Although all of the words in the list have the **al** ending, it is not always a suffix to a root word e.g. if we remove the **al** from the word *hospital* we find *hospit*, which is not a word in itself. However, if we remove the **al** from the word *musical* we find *music*, which is a word. The activity on Worksheet 8 helps the students with this concept. Note that words such as *arrival* and *central* are slightly more difficult as their root words have a letter **e** in place of **al**.

- To analyse the words further, and if appropriate for your students, you could complete the following activities.

  Segmenting the words into their phonemes
  Explain to the students that they are going to segment some of the words into their separate sounds. Demonstrate this with the word *central* by drawing lines between the graphemes that represent the separate phonemes: /c/e/n/t/r/a/l/. Note that in this word every letter represents a separate sound. Discuss the sounds, particularly the letter **c**, making the phoneme /s/, and **a** making the phoneme /u/.

  Splitting the words into their syllables (syllabification)
  For most students syllabification is much easier than segmenting. Explain that they are now going to split the words into 'chunks' of sound and give the example of *decimal*: \de\cim\al\. Can the students hear that the word can be split into three syllables? Point out that each syllable normally contains at least one vowel.

2 Words in context

- When the students are ready ask them to complete the second activity on the worksheet.

musical	electrical	medical	seasonal
arrival	annual	central	decimal
emotional	equal	festival	final
historical	hospital	local	material

Words ending in al

Name _____

1 Write the focus words in the spaces on this grid.

Some of the **al** words are made from shorter words e.g. music ⟶ musical

An ending added to a word to change its meaning is called a suffix.
The suffix **al** can be added to the word music.

Add the suffix **al** to the following words:

music _____   centre _____

electric _____   emotion _____

medic _____   festive _____

season _____   history _____

arrive _____   (another one to be very careful with!)

(be very careful with this one!)

Now write the other **al** words from the grid.

_____ _____ _____

_____ _____ _____ _____

2 Write the missing words in the sentences below.

He played the guitar very well because he is so _____ .

She announced the _____ of the train at the _____ station.

Is the _____ 0.5 _____ to the fraction one half?

She won the _____ of the competition.

He went to _____ for a _____ examination.

Words beginning with al

1 Focus on words

- Photocopy this page and the accompanying student worksheet. Discuss the focus words at the bottom of this page with the students. Ask them to write the words in the blank grid on their worksheet. You could dictate the words or, if appropriate, students could copy them from the set below.

- The completed grid on the worksheet, or the one below, could be laminated as a pocket reference card that students could refer to later.

- Discuss some of the words in more detail, asking the students which ones are a combination of the word **all** and a different word e.g. *already* is derived from 'all ready'; *altogether* is derived from 'all together'. Note that this is not true for all of the words. Discuss the words *all right* with the students. Some grammarians would not accept 'alright' as correct. However, modern usage now allows 'alright'.

- To analyse the words further, and if appropriate for your students, you could complete the following activities.

  Segmenting the words into their phonemes
  Explain to the students that they are going to segment some of the words into their separate sounds. Demonstrate this with the word *always* by drawing lines between the graphemes that represent the separate phonemes: /a/l/w/ay/s/. Students may come up with different answers from each other but the important part of the activity is the process of hearing the sounds and observing how they are represented by graphemes.

  Splitting the words into their syllables (syllabification)
  For most students syllabification is much easier than segmenting. Explain that they are now going to split the words into 'chunks' of sound and give the example of *already*: \al\read\y\. Can the students hear that the word can be split into three syllables? Point out that each syllable normally contains at least one vowel.

2 Words in context

- When the students are ready ask them to complete the second activity on the worksheet in one of two ways. They can either attempt to read the sentences themselves and write the missing words or they can listen to you dictating the sentences and write the missing words as you dictate them.

almost	also	along	always
already	altogether	allergy	allowed
aloud	algebra	alphabet	alarm
alien	alligator	alternating	alike

Words beginning with **al**

Name _____

1 Write the focus words in the spaces on this grid.

All the words begin with **al**. Some of them have **double l**. Write the words that have **double l**.

_____   _____   _____

Look at these two words: *aloud* and *allowed*. They both sound the same but they are spelt differently and they mean different things. Words like these are called homophones.

2 Write the correct word in each of these sentences:

She had to read the poem _____ .

He was not _____ to stay up late.

The last letter of the _____ is z.

In maths we are working on _____ .

The power supply is an _____ current.

How is an _____ different from a crocodile?

Now look at these words: *all right   alright*
A few years ago you would be criticised for writing *alright* when you should have written *all right* but language changes and these days most people are happy with *alright*.

So … it's all right to write alright!

Write a sentence using at least two words that begin with **al**.

_____

_____

Present and past vocabulary

1 Focus on words

- Photocopy this page and the accompanying student worksheet. Discuss the focus words at the bottom of this page with the students. Ask them to write the words in the blank grid on their worksheet. You could dictate the words or, if appropriate, students could copy them from the set below.

- The completed grid on the worksheet, or the one below, could be laminated as a pocket reference card that students could refer to later.

- The creation of past tense words has already been considered on Worksheet 7, specifically in looking at words ending in **ed** but also in examining some words that change from present to past tense in different ways. The activity on Worksheet 10 provides revision of **ed** words and some of the exceptions as well as providing practice of a valuable set of high frequency words.

- To analyse the words further, and if appropriate, you could complete the following two activities with the students.

Segmenting the words into their phonemes
Explain to the students that they are going to segment some of the words into their separate sounds. Demonstrate this with the word *ask* by drawing lines between the graphemes that represent the separate phonemes: /a/s/k/. Now look at *asked*: /a/s/k/ed/. They may come up with different answers from each other but the important part of the activity is the process of hearing the separate sounds and observing how they are represented by graphemes.

Splitting the words into their syllables (syllabification)
For most students syllabification is much easier than segmenting. Explain that they are now going to split the words into 'chunks' of sound and look again at *asked*: \asked\. Can the students hear that the word has only one syllable, the same as the word *ask*? Now look at *start* and ask the students to compare it to *started*. Point out that each syllable normally contains at least one vowel.

2 Writing past tense words

- When the students are ready ask them to complete the second activity on the worksheet which involves writing the past tense of selected words.

tell	think	ask	bring
change	hear	jump	know
open	own	show	start
stop	swim	try	turn
walk	watch	wake	write

Present and past vocabulary

Name _____

1 Write the focus words in the spaces on this grid.

We have already looked at present and past on Worksheet 7. Have another look at the words on that sheet.

2 Now look carefully at the words at the very bottom of this page. When you think you know how to spell them fold the paper over so that you can't see them, then complete the activity below.

Write the past tense word for each of these present tense words.

tell	_____	show	_____
think	_____	start	_____
ask	_____	stop	_____
bring	_____	swim	_____
change	_____	try	_____
hear	_____	turn	_____
jump	_____	walk	_____
know	_____	watch	_____
open	_____	wake	_____
own	_____	write	_____

- -

Fold here when you are ready.

brought   showed   knew   walked   started   swam   owned
changed   wrote   opened   tried   thought   asked
heard   turned   told   jumped   watched   stopped   woke

Contractions

1 Focus on words

● Photocopy this page and the accompanying student worksheet. Discuss the focus words at the bottom of this page with the students. Ask them to write the words in the blank grid on their worksheet. You could dictate the words or, if appropriate, students could copy them from the set below.

● The completed grid on the worksheet, or the one below, could be laminated as a pocket reference card that students could refer to later.

● Discuss some of the words in more detail. Many contractions are easy to understand e.g. it is easy to see that *it's* is contracted from *it is* and that the apostrophe is written where the letter **i** has been omitted. Ask the students to identify the words where more than one letter has been omitted: *I've, you've, can't*. One of the most difficult words to deal with is *won't*, which of course comes from *will not*.

● To analyse the words further, and if appropriate for your students, you may like to complete the following activities.

Segmenting the words into their phonemes
Explain to the students that they are going to segment some of the words into separate sounds. Demonstrate this with the word *didn't* by drawing lines between the graphemes that represent the phonemes: /d/i/d/n'/t/. Now look at *you've*: /y/ou/'ve/. In examining the words students may come up with different answers from each other but the important part of the activity is the process of hearing the sounds and observing how they are represented by graphemes.

Syllabification
For most students syllabification is much easier than segmenting. Explain that they are now going to split the words into 'chunks' of sound and look again at *wouldn't*: \would\n't\. Can the students hear that the word can be split into two syllables?

2 Practising contracted forms

● When the students are ready ask them to complete the second activity on the worksheet.

I'm	can't	didn't	don't
won't	couldn't	shouldn't	they're
it's	I've	you've	you're
she's	he's	wouldn't	haven't

Contractions

Name _____

1 Write the focus words in the spaces on this grid.

When we speak we often squash two words together and letters get missed out. E.g. we are more likely to say, "**I'm** not going out tonight," than "**I am** not going out tonight". We use the word *I'm* in place of the two words *I am*, and the letter **a** has been missed out so we replace it with an apostrophe.

2 Match the contracted words below with the words that they represent. The first one has been done for you.

'contracted form'	'not contracted form'	'contracted form'	'not contracted form'
I'm	do not	it's	you have
can't	they are	I've	you are
didn't	will not	you've	she is
don't	I am	you're	it is
won't	should not	she's	he is
couldn't	did not	he's	I have
shouldn't	could not	wouldn't	have not
they're	can not	haven't	would not

Write a sentence using as many contracted words as possible.

_____

_____

_____

Months and seasons

1 Focus on words

- Photocopy this page and the accompanying student worksheet. Discuss the focus words at the bottom of this page with the students. Ask them to write the words in the blank grid on their worksheet. You could dictate the words or, if appropriate, students could copy them from the set below.

- The completed grid on the worksheet, or the one below, could be laminated as a pocket reference card that students could refer to later.

- Discuss some of the words in more detail, particularly of course *February*. Take the opportunity to look at the word *library*, which also contains **br**. Encourage the students to say the words clearly: *Feb ru ary li bra ry*.

- Discuss also the word *season's*, pointing out that it contains an apostrophe. This time the apostrophe is not replacing a missing letter but is doing the other job of an apostrophe: showing possession or ownership or belonging. We write 'season's greetings' because the greetings are 'of the season' or 'belong to the season'.

- To analyse the words further, and if appropriate for your students, you could complete the following activities.

Segmenting the words into their phonemes

This is not an easy activity but the process encourages students to listen closely to the sounds that constitute the words. Explain to the students that they are going to segment some of the words into their separate sounds. Demonstrate this with the word *February* by drawing lines between the graphemes that represent the separate phonemes: */F/e/b/r/u/ar/y/*. In examining the words, students may come up with different answers from each other but the important part of the activity is the process of hearing the separate sounds and observing how they are represented by graphemes.

Splitting the words into their syllables (syllabification)

For most students syllabification is much easier than segmenting. Explain that they are now going to split the words into 'chunks' of sound and give the example of *February* again: \Feb\ru\a\ry\. Can the students hear that the word can be split into four syllables?

2 Words in context

- When the students are ready ask them to complete the second activity on the worksheets which asks them to think about 'special months'. You could prompt them with ideas such as their birthday month, a family member's birthday month, the month Christmas is in, etc.

May	February	October	August
April	December	June	September
July	January	November	March
autumn	winter	spring	summer
season	season's	greetings	seasonal

Months and seasons

Name _____

1 Write the focus words in the spaces on this grid.

Write the months of the year in the correct order.

_____   _____

_____   _____

_____   _____

_____   _____

_____   _____

_____   _____

2 Choose three months that are special to you in some way. Write a sentence about why each month is special.

_____

_____

_____

_____

_____

_____

_____

_____

Compound words

Learning objective:
Spelling compound words

1 Focus on words

- Photocopy this page and the accompanying student worksheet. Discuss the focus words at the bottom of this page with the students. (Some of the words have appeared on previous sheets). Ask the students to write the words in the blank grid on their worksheet. You could dictate the words or, if appropriate, students could copy them from the set below.

- The completed grid on the worksheet, or the one below, could be laminated as a pocket reference card that students could refer to later.

- Explain to the students that compound words are single words made from two others joined together. Point out that all of the focus words are compound words and that each one is made of two words joined together without losing any letters e.g. *some* and *thing* make *something*. (Note that many pupils write *somthing*.)

- To analyse the words further, and if appropriate for your students, you could complete the following activities.

  Segmenting the words into their phonemes
  Explain to the students that they are going to segment some of the words into their separate sounds. Demonstrate this with the word *anything* by drawing lines between the graphemes that represent the separate phonemes e.g. */a/n/y/th/i/ng/*. In examining the words students may come up with different answers from each other but the important part of the activity is the process of hearing the separate sounds and observing how they are represented by graphemes.

  Splitting the words into their syllables (syllabification)
  For most students syllabification is much easier than segmenting. Explain that they are now going to split the words into 'chunks' of sound and give the example of *sometimes*: \some\times\. Can the students hear how the word can be split into two syllables?

2 Words in context

- When the students are ready ask them to complete the second activity on the worksheet.

anywhere	anybody	anything	anyway
somewhere	somebody	somehow	someone
something	sometimes	everybody	everyday
everything	everyone	everywhere	birthday
birthplace	overall	overbalance	overboard

Compound words

Name _____

1 Write the focus words in the spaces on this grid.
All of the words are compound words. They are single words made from two others joined together.

2 Draw lines to join the words on the left to all the words on the right that will combine with them to make compound words.

	where
	body
any	thing
	way
some	how
	one
every	times
	day
birth	place
	all
over	balance
	board

Write a sentence containing as many compound words as possible. It doesn't matter how crazy your sentence is but make sure it is a full sentence.

_____

_____

_____

Words containing **ou**

Learning objective: Spelling words containing **ou**

1 Focus on words

- Photocopy this page and the accompanying student worksheet. Discuss the focus words at the bottom of this page with the students. Ask the students to write the words in the blank grid on their worksheet. You could dictate the words or, if appropriate, students could copy them from the set below.

- The completed grid on the worksheet, or the one below, could be laminated as a pocket reference card that students could refer to later.

- Discuss some of the words in more detail. Look at the word *thousand*. Many students find this word difficult. You could provide the following mnemonic: there are thousands of grains of sand on the beach: *thou sand*.

- To analyse the words further, and if appropriate for your students, you could complete the following activities.

  Segmenting the words into their phonemes
  Explain to the students that they are going to segment some of the words into their separate sounds. Demonstrate this with the word *thousand* by drawing lines between the graphemes that represent the separate phonemes e.g. /th/ou/s/a/n/d/. In examining the words, students may come up with different answers from each other but the important part of the activity is the process of hearing the separate sounds and observing how they are represented by graphemes.

  Splitting the words into their syllables (syllabification)
  For most students syllabification is much easier than segmenting. Explain that they are now going to split the words into 'chunks' of sound and give the example of *counting*: \count\ing\. Can the students hear that the word can be split into two syllables?

2 Words in context

- When the students are ready ask them to complete the second activity on the worksheet.

found	sound	ground	pound
around	bounce	pounce	lounge
count	counter	counting	thousand
mountain	fountain	trousers	outside
without	wound	mound	bouncing

Words containing **ou**

Name _____

1 Write the focus words in the spaces on this grid.

Look at the words **pounce** and **pound**. Both of the words begin with the letters **p o u n**. If we want to write the words in alphabetical order we have to look at the next letter. We can see that **pounce** must be written before **pound** because **c** comes before **d** in the alphabet.

Try to write the twenty words in alphabetical order.

_____ _____

_____ _____

_____ _____

_____ _____

_____ _____

_____ _____

_____ _____

_____ _____

_____ _____

_____ _____

2 Write a sentence containing as many **ou** words as possible.

_____

_____

_____

_____

Words beginning with **wh**

1 Focus on words

● Photocopy this page and the accompanying student worksheet. Discuss the focus words at the bottom of the page with the students. Ask them to write the words in the blank grid on their worksheet. You could dictate the words or, if appropriate, students could copy them from the set below.

● The completed grid on the worksheet, or the one below, could be laminated as a pocket reference card that students could refer to later.

● Discuss some of the words in more detail. Point out that the grapheme *wh* can create the phoneme /w/ in words such as *where*, with a silent **h**, but that the phoneme will be /wh/ in the same word in some parts of the country. Notice also that in some of the words the grapheme *wh* gives the phoneme /h/, with a silent **w**, in words such as *whole* or *who* or *whooping*.

● To analyse the words further, and if appropriate for your students, you could complete the following activities.

Segmenting the words into their phonemes
Explain to the students that they are going to segment some of the words into their separate sounds. Demonstrate with the word *where* by drawing lines between the graphemes that represent the separate phonemes: /wh/ere/. This is quite a difficult word to separate into sounds as in most parts of the country it only has the two phonemes /w/ and /air/. In examining the words the students may come up with different answers from each other but the important part of the activity is the process of hearing the separate sounds and observing how they are represented by graphemes.

Splitting the words into their syllables (syllabification)
For most students syllabification is much easier than segmenting. Explain that they are now going to split the words into 'chunks' of sound and give the example of *whatever*: \what\e\ver\. Can the students hear that the word can be split into three syllables?

2 Words in context

● When the students are ready ask them to complete the second activity on the worksheet, which encourages them to focus on question words which begin with **wh**.

where	while	white	whole
when	what	whenever	whatever
wherever	why	wheel	wheelbarrow
wheelchair	which	whichever	whistle
whisper	whispered	whereabouts	whisker

Words beginning with **wh**

Name _____

1 Write the focus words in the spaces on this grid.

2 Lots of words begin with **wh**. Lots of question words begin with **wh**. Try to decide which **wh** words can be written at the start of these question sentences:

_____ did the chicken cross the road?

_____ is your name?

_____ are you going to do your homework?

_____ are you going on holiday?

_____ way is it to Oxford Street?

Now write three question sentences of your own. Include a **wh** word in each sentence.

_____

_____

_____

_____

_____

_____

_____

_____

Words beginning with un

1 Focus on words

- Photocopy this page and the accompanying student worksheet. Discuss the focus words at the bottom of the page with the students. Ask them to write the words in the blank grid on their worksheet. You could dictate the words or, if appropriate, students could copy them from the set below.

- The completed grid on the worksheet, or the one below, could be laminated as a pocket reference card that students could refer to later.

- Discuss some of the words in more detail. It is helpful to explain to the students that **un** is a prefix that is added to an existing word to make a new words with a different meaning. Point out that the spelling is not changed by adding the prefix **un** e.g. **un** can be added to *necessary* and the new word will keep the letter **n** from each part: *unnecessary*.

- To analyse the words further, and if appropriate for your students, you could complete the following activities.

  Segmenting the words into their phonemes
  Explain to the students that they are going to segment some of the words into their separate sounds. Demonstrate with the word *unafraid* by drawing lines between the graphemes that represent the separate phonemes: /u/n/a/f/r/ai/d/. In examining the words, students may come up with different answers from each other but the important part of the activity is the process of hearing the separate sounds and observing how they are represented by graphemes.

  Splitting the words into their syllables (syllabification)
  For most students syllabification is much easier than segmenting. Explain that they are now going to split the words into 'chunks' of sound and give the example of *unenthusiastic*: \un\en\thu\si\as\tic\. Can the students hear how the word can be split into six syllables? Now look at *unfortunately* and ask the students to compare it to *unfortunate*.

2 Words in context

- When the students are ready ask them to complete the second activity on the worksheet, which reminds the students that removing the prefix from a word can create the antonym.

unable	unadventurous	unafraid	unanswered
unassisted	unavailable	unavoidable	unchanged
uncomfortable	unconnected	uncool	unenjoyable
unenthusiastic	unequal	unfair	unfinished
unforgettable	unfortunately	unfriendly	unnecessary

Words beginning with un

Name _____

1 Write the focus words in the spaces on this grid.

The two letters **u** and **n** can be added to the front of lots of words to turn them into opposites e.g. **necessary** means 'a need to do something'. When we put the prefix **un** on to the word **necessary** we get the word **unnecessary** which means 'no need to do something'.

Look at these words in sentences:

The doctor found it **necessary** to send the patient to hospital.

The visit to hospital was **unnecessary** because the patient recovered quickly.

2 Choose one of the **un** words from the grid and work out its opposite.
Write a sentence for each of the words.

_____

_____

_____

_____

Now choose another **un** word and its opposite. Write a sentence for each of the words.

_____

_____

_____

_____

Words beginning with under

1 Focus on words

- Photocopy this page and the accompanying student worksheet. Discuss the focus words at the bottom of the page with the students. Ask them to write the words in the blank grid on their worksheet. You could dictate the words or, if appropriate, students could copy them from the set below.

- The completed grid on the worksheet, or the one below, could be laminated as a pocket reference card that students could refer to later.

- The focus words on this page are all compound words, each created from the word *under* together with another complete word. The activities provide opportunities to look closely at these other complete words.

- To analyse the words further, and if appropriate for your students, you could complete the following activities.

Segmenting the words into their phonemes
Explain to the students that they are going to segment some of the words into their separate sounds. Demonstrate with the word *undercoat* by drawing lines between the graphemes that represent the separate phonemes: /u/n/d/er/c/oa/t/. In examining the words students may come up with different answers from each other but the important part of the activity is in the process of listening to the sounds and observing how they are represented by graphemes.

Splitting the words into their syllables (syllabification)
For most students syllabification is much easier than segmenting. Explain that they are now going to split the words into 'chunks' of sound and give the example of *undercover*: \un\der\co\ver\. Can the students hear that the word can be split into four syllables?

2 Words in context

- When the students are ready ask them to complete the second activity on the worksheet, which encourages them to experiment with the words by attempting to replace *under* with *over*.

undercarriage	undercharge	undercoat	undercover
underdeveloped	underestimate	underfed	underfloor
underfoot	underground	undergrowth	underneath
underpaid	underpass	underpowered	undersea
understand	understood	underwater	undercut

Words beginning with under

Name _____

1 Write the focus words in the spaces on this grid.

Each of the focus words is a compound word made from the word **under** together with another word. In many of them we could replace **under** with **over** and make a new compound word.

Look again at each of the words below. If you can make a new word starting with **over**, write your new word on the line. If you cannot make a new word, draw a cross on the line.

undercarriage	_____	undergrowth	_____
undercharge	_____	underneath	_____
undercoat	_____	underpaid	_____
undercover	_____	underpass	_____
underdeveloped	_____	underpowered	_____
underestimate	_____	undersea	_____
underfed	_____	understand	_____
underfloor	_____	understood	_____
underfoot	_____	underwater	_____
underground	_____	undercut	_____

2 Try to write a sentence that contains an **under** word and an **over** word.

_____

_____

Words beginning with dis

1 Focus on words

- Photocopy this page and the accompanying student worksheet. Discuss the focus words at the bottom of the page with the students. Ask them to write the words in the blank grid on their worksheet. You could dictate the words or, if appropriate, students could copy them from the set below.

- The completed grid on the worksheet, or the one below, could be laminated as a pocket reference card that students could refer to later.

- Discuss some of the words in more detail. It is helpful to explain to the students that for some of the words **dis** is a prefix that is added to existing words to make new words with a different meaning e.g. *honest* becomes its opposite *dishonest* when **dis** is added. However, for many of the focus words **dis** is not a modern prefix and so the removal of **dis** will not reveal another related word e.g. removing **dis** from *disaster* reveals *aster*, which is the name of a flower! (Note, however, that the word *disaster* comes from the Italian *disastro*, which in turn comes from the Latin *dis astrum* and so the **dis** can be seen as an 'ancient' prefix. This is probably not relevant to your students!)

- To analyse the words further, and if appropriate for your students, you could complete the following activities.

  Segmenting the words into their phonemes
  .Explain to the students that they are going to segment some of the words into their separate sounds. Demonstrate with the word *disallow* by drawing lines between the graphemes that represent the separate phonemes: /d/i/s/a/ll/ow/. In examining the words students may come up with different answers from each other but the important part of the activity is the process of listening to the sounds and observing how they are represented by graphemes.

  Splitting the words into their syllables (syllabification)
  For most students syllabification is much easier than segmenting. Explain that they are now going to split the words into 'chunks' of sound and give the example of *disallow*: \dis\a\llow\. Can the students hear how the word can be split into three syllables?

2 Words in context

- When the students are ready ask them to complete the second activity on the worksheet, which reminds the students that removing the prefix from a word can create the antonym.

disappear	disallow	dishonest	disappoint
disadvantage	disagree	disapprove	disaster
discount	discover	discuss	disguise
disgust	disinfect	disintegrate	dislike
dislocate	disorder	dispersal	disqualify

Words beginning with dis

Name _____

1 Write the focus words in the spaces on this grid.

In some of the focus words the prefix **dis** has been added to another word to change its meaning e.g. **disappear** has the prefix **dis** added to the word **appear** to create the opposite.

Look carefully again at each of the focus words. Next to each word, if possible, write its opposite without the prefix **dis**. If you cannot make a word that means the opposite, draw a cross on the line.

disappear _____ discuss _____

disallow _____ disguise _____

dishonest _____ disgust _____

disappoint _____ disinfect _____

disadvantage _____ disintegrate _____

disagree _____ dislike _____

disapprove _____ dislocate _____

disaster _____ disorder _____

discount _____ dispersal _____

discover _____ disqualify _____

2 Try to write a sentence that contains two **dis** words.

_____

_____

Words containing th

Learning objective: To understand the use of the two sounds made by **th**

1 Focus on words

● Photocopy this page and the accompanying student worksheet. Discuss the focus words at the bottom of the page with the students. Ask them to write the words in the blank grid on their worksheet. You could dictate the words or, if appropriate, students could copy them from the set below.

● The completed grid on the worksheet, or the one below, could be laminated as a pocket reference card that students could refer to later.

● Help the students to read the words aloud and to analyse the sounds that they can hear, encouraging them to notice that the grapheme **th** can make the hard /th/ phoneme as in *the* or the soft /th/ phoneme as in *thin*. This is the focus for the activity on the second part of the worksheet.

● To analyse the words further, and if appropriate for your students, you could complete the following activities.

Segmenting the words into their phonemes

Explain to the students that they are going to segment some of the words into their separate sounds. The process of segmenting will reveal the two different sounds given by the grapheme **th**. Demonstrate with the word *together* by drawing lines between the graphemes that represent the separate phonemes: /t/o/g/e/th/er/. Now look at *truthful*: /t/r/u/th/f/u/l/. In examining the words students may come up with different answers from each other but the important part of the activity is in the process of listening to the sounds and observing how they are represented by graphemes particularly the grapheme **th**.

Splitting the words into their syllables (syllabification)

For most students syllabification is much easier than segmenting. Explain that they are now going to split the words into 'chunks' of sound and give the example of *together*: \to\ge\ther\. Can the students hear that the word can be split into three syllables? Note, however, that some of the words are more difficult e.g. the word *thought* only has one syllable and it only has three phonemes /th/, /or/ and /t/ represented by the graphemes **th**, **ough** and **t**. The word *rhythm* is particularly interesting as it has two syllables but no vowels. It is worth reminding students that usually each syllable contains at least one vowel.

2 Words in context

● When the students are ready ask them to complete the second activity on the worksheet.

those	clothes	truthfully	together
there	through	they're	weather
cloth	moth	thought	both
their	mouth	youth	truth
truthful	though	myth	rhythm

Words containing **th**

Name _____

1 Write the focus words in the spaces on this grid.

Say each of the focus words. Can you hear the different sounds that **th** makes? Sort the words into two groups. One group should contain the words with the hard **th** sound, like **the**. The other group should contain the words with the soft **th** sound, like **moth**.

hard th	soft th

2 Look at these words: **they're   there   their**

These three words are homophones. They all sound the same but they are spelt differently and they mean different things:

> **they're** is a contraction of the words **they are**
> **there** is always to do with a place or position
> **their** is always to do with some people owning something

Choose the correct word to fit into each of the sentences below.

I live over _____ .

I like _____ house.

I wonder when _____ going to move.

Words containing ight

Learning objective: Spelling words containing the graphemes **ight**

1 Focus on words

- Photocopy this page and the accompanying student worksheet. Discuss the focus words at the bottom of the page with the students. Ask them to write the words in the blank grid on their worksheet. You could dictate the words or, if appropriate, students could copy them from the set below.

- The completed grid on the worksheet, or the one below, could be laminated as a pocket reference card that students could refer to later.

- Discuss some of the words in more detail. All of the words contain the letter string **ight** but in some of them the letter string is extended to *eight* e.g. *eight*, *weight* and *height*. Can the students hear that the *eight* is making a different sound in *eight* and *weight* from the one it makes in *height*?

- Point out the word *delightful*, explaining that the suffix **ful** has been added to the word *delight* to mean 'full of delight'. An extension activity would be to ask students to think of other words with the suffix **ful**.

- To analyse the words further, and if appropriate for your students, you could complete the following activities.

  Segmenting the words into their phonemes
  Explain to the students that they are going to segment some of the words into their separate sounds. Demonstrate with the word *lightning* by drawing lines between the graphemes that represent the separate phonemes: /l/igh/t/n/i/ng/. In examining the words students may come up with different answers from each other but the important part of the activity is in the process of listening to the sounds and observing how they are represented by graphemes.

  Splitting the words into their syllables (syllabification)
  For most students syllabification is much easier than segmenting. Explain that they are now going to split the words into 'chunks' of sound and give the example of *lightning* again: \light\ning\. Can the students hear that the word can be split into two syllables?

2 Word puzzle

- When the students are ready ask them to do the second activity which involves completing a word puzzle using the focus words.

light	lighting	lightning	delight
delightful	bright	right	might
fight	flight	fright	sight
height	eight	straight	slight
night	knight	weight	freight

Words containing ight

Name _____

1 Write the focus words in the spaces on this grid.

2 Use the clues to complete the word puzzle.

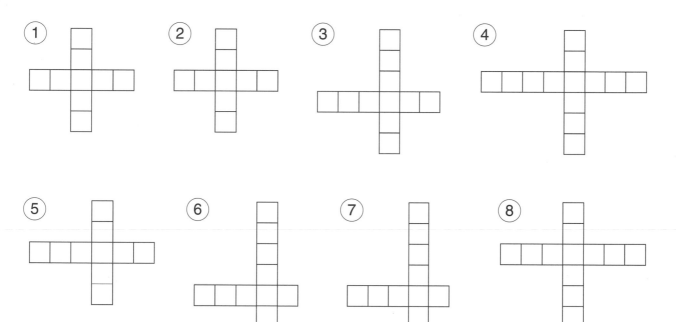

Clues Across

1) Opposite of left
2) Not day
3) Distance above the ground
4) Not bendy
5) A medieval soldier
6) Ability to see
7) Maybe
8) Cargo

Clues Down

1) Fisticuffs
2) Not dark
3) Going through the air
4) A scare
5) One more than seven
6) Intelligent
7) A slim build
8) Heaviness.

Plurals created by adding es

1 Focus on words

- Photocopy this page and the accompanying student worksheet. Discuss the focus words at the bottom of the page with the students. Ask them to write the words in the blank grid on their worksheet. You could dictate the words or, if appropriate, students could copy them from the set below.

- The completed grid on the worksheet, or the one below, could be laminated as a pocket reference card that students could refer to later.

- Discuss some of the words in more detail e.g. compare the words *peaches* and *pitches*. Both have similar sounds but one contains **ch** and the other has **tch**. Which other words have the grapheme **ch** and which have the grapheme **tch**? Are the two sounds the same? Can the students hear the /t/ phoneme in the words with the grapheme **tch**?

- To analyse the words further, and if appropriate for your students, you could complete the following activities.

  Segmenting the words into their phonemes
  Explain to the students that they are going to segment some of the words into their separate sounds. Demonstrate with the word *crashes* by drawing lines between the graphemes that represent the separate phonemes: /c/r/a/sh/e/s/. In examining the words students may come up with different answers from each other but the important part of the activity is the process of hearing the separate sounds and observing how they are represented by graphemes.

  Splitting the words into their syllables (syllabification)
  For most students syllabification is much easier than segmenting. Explain that they are now going to split the words into 'chunks' of sound and give the example of *stitches*: \stitch\es\. Can the students hear that the word can be split into two syllables? The syllabification process makes all of these words easier to spell. The students should be able to hear that creating the plural of each word adds an extra syllable and therefore needs an extra vowel.

2 Words in context

- When the students are ready ask them to complete the second activity on the worksheet, in one of two ways. They can either attempt to read the sentences themselves and write the missing words or they can listen to you dictating the sentences and write the missing words as you dictate them.

watches	rushes	crashes	matches
brushes	stitches	witches	catches
dishes	beaches	rashes	churches
crutches	riches	pitches	peaches
sandwiches	pitches	eyelashes	patches

Plurals created by adding es

Name _____

1 Write the focus words in the spaces on this grid.

Complete the table below. Label the pictures correctly.

Singular	Plural	Singular	Plural
watch _____	_____	witch _____	_____
crash _____	_____	_____	rashes _____
_____	dishes _____	pitch _____	_____
_____	crutches _____	match _____	_____
stitch _____	_____	_____	catches _____
beach _____	_____	church _____	_____
brushes _____	_____	peach _____	_____

2 Write the missing words in these sentences.

Her cut needed four _____ .

Near their hotel were two golden sandy _____ .

When washing up the best _____ he took great care.

There are three _____ in the town.

There are several _____ on the dressing table in the bedroom.

The playing field had four football _____ which were used each week.

While his leg was healing he used _____ to help him walk.

Most people keep a box of _____ in their home.

Plurals ending in ves

1 Focus on words

- Photocopy this page and the accompanying student worksheet. Discuss the focus words at the bottom of the page with the students. Ask them to write the words in the blank grid on their worksheet. You could dictate the words or, if appropriate, students could copy them from the set below.

- The completed grid on the worksheet, or the one below, could be laminated as a pocket reference card that students could refer to later.

- These plural words present a surprising amount of difficulty to many students. By saying the words and listening to the phonemes the students should be able to hear that the /f/ phoneme changes to /v/. Encourage them to notice that the plural contains the letter **e** before the final **s**, unlike words such as *match* and *matches*, where the letter **e** can be heard as part of the second syllable. These plurals are all single syllable words.

- To analyse the words further, and if appropriate for your students, you could complete the following activities.

  Segmenting the words into their phonemes
  Explain to the students that they are going to segment some of the words into their separate sounds. Demonstrate with the word *knife* by drawing lines between the graphemes that represent the separate phonemes: /kn/i/fe/. Hopefully the students will notice that the letter **k** is silent. Now look at *knives*: /kn/i/v/es/. In examining the words students may come up with different answers from each other but the important part of the activity is the process of listening to the sounds and observing how they are represented by graphemes.

  Splitting the words into their syllables (syllabification)
  Syllabification is not particularly helpful with this set of words, though that fact should be discussed with the students. They are all single syllable words, even in the plural form where the ending **es** is not adding an extra syllable.

2 Words in context

- When the students are ready ask them to complete the second activity on the worksheet.

knife	knives	scarf	scarves
wife	wives	shelf	shelves
wolf	wolves	loaf	loaves
leaf	leaves	half	halves
life	lives	calf	calves

Plurals ending in ves

Name _____

1 Write the focus words in the spaces on this grid.

Most words ending with an **f** sound have the ending **ves** in the plural.
Read each of the words below. Write the plurals on the lines provided.

Singular	Plural		Singular	Plural
knife	_____		life	_____
wife	_____		scarf	_____
elf	_____		shelf	_____
loaf	_____		half	_____
wolf	_____		calf	_____
leaf	_____		hoof	_____

2 Write the missing words in these sentences.

She put three _____, three forks and three spoons on the table.

The man took his _____ on holiday.

There was a pack of _____ in the forest.

Dad put some new _____ on the wall.

She ate _____ the sweets and saved the rest until later.

The baker baked twenty fresh _____ of bread every morning.

Each autumn he watched the _____ falling from the trees.

It was a cold day, so she wrapped her warm woolly _____ around her neck.

Plurals of words ending in y

1 Focus on words

- Photocopy this page and the accompanying student worksheet. Discuss the focus words at the bottom of the page with the students. Ask them to write the words in the blank grid on their worksheet. You could dictate the words or, if appropriate, students could copy them from the set below.

- The completed grid on the worksheet, or the one below, could be laminated as a pocket reference card that students could refer to later.

- Discuss the rule with the students: if there is no vowel before the **y**, remove the **y** and write **ies**. The corresponding rule is that if there is a vowel before the **y**, just add **s** to make the plural.

- To analyse the words further, and if appropriate for your students, you could complete the following activities.

Segmenting the words into their phonemes
Explain to the students that they are going to segment some of the words into their separate sounds. Demonstrate with the word *ponies* by drawing lines between the graphemes that represent the separate phonemes: /p/o/n/ie/s/. In examining the words students may come up with different answers from each other but the important part of the activity is the process of listening to the sounds and observing how they are represented by graphemes.

Splitting the words into their syllables (syllabification)
For most students syllabification is much easier than segmenting. Explain that they are now going to split the words into 'chunks' of sound and give the example of *pony*: \po\ny\. Point out that usually each syllable needs at least one vowel but that here the consonant **y** is acting as a vowel. Now look at *berry* and ask the students to compare it to *berries*.

2 Words in context

- When the students are ready ask them to complete the second activity on the worksheet, in one of two ways. They can either attempt to read the sentences themselves and write the missing words or they can listen to you dictating the sentences and write the missing words as you dictate them.

pony	ponies	valley	valleys
berry	berries	cry	cries
cherry	cherries	baby	babies
fly	flies	tray	trays
holiday	holidays	enemy	enemies

Plurals of words ending in y

1 Write the focus words in the spaces on this grid.

Look at these words and their plurals.

carry   carries   play   plays

Remember the rule that if there is no vowel in front of the **y**, then change the **y** to **i** and add **es**. Complete the chart below.

Singular	Plural	Singular	Plural
pony	_____	baby	_____
valley	_____	spy	_____
_____	berries	_____	rays
_____	cherries	enemy	_____
_____	trays	_____	ferries
fly	_____	try	_____
cry	_____	_____	keys

2 Write the missing words in these sentences.

They rode over mountains and through _____ .

A herd of _____ trotted over the field.

She loved eating _____ fresh from the tree.

The _____ cried because they needed feeding.

Their _____ were very loud.

The waiters took _____ of drink to the guests.

They liked to pick black _____ from the hedge in the autumn.

Three large _____ buzzed around the light.

Words containing gh or ph

Learning objective: Spelling words containing **gh** or **ph**

1 Focus on words

- Photocopy this page and the accompanying student worksheet. Discuss the focus words at the bottom of the page with the students. Ask them to write the words in the blank grid on their worksheet. You could dictate the words or, if appropriate, students could copy them from the set below.

- The completed grid on the worksheet, or the one below, could be laminated as a pocket reference card that students could refer to later.

- Discuss some of the words in more detail. You could ask the students to sort them into two lists – words that contain **gh** and words that contain **ph**. Point out that in both lists the sound made by the **gh** and the **ph** is /f/.

- To analyse the words further, and if appropriate for your students, you could complete the following activities.

Segmenting the words into their phonemes
Explain to the students that they are going to segment some of the words into their separate sounds. Demonstrate with the word *sphere* by drawing lines between the graphemes that represent the separate phonemes: */s/ph/ere/*. In examining the words students may come up with different answers from each other but the important part of the activity is the process of listening to the sounds and observing how they are represented by graphemes.

Splitting the words into their syllables (syllabification)
For most students syllabification is much easier than segmenting. Explain that they are now going to split the words into 'chunks' of sound and give the example of *photograph*: \pho\to\graph\. Can the students hear that the word can be split into three syllables? Can they see that this word contains **ph** twice?

2 Words in context

- When the students are ready ask them to complete the second activity on the worksheet, in one of two ways. They can either attempt to read the sentences themselves and write the missing words or they can listen to you dictating the sentences and write the missing words as you dictate them.

sphere	alphabet	catastrophe	geography
cough	trough	rough	tough
graph	physical	photograph	telephone
autograph	biography	laugh	enough
photographer	photographic	autobiography	catastrophic

Words containing gh or ph

Name _____

1 Write the focus words in the spaces on this grid.

Choose words from the grid to complete the puzzle.

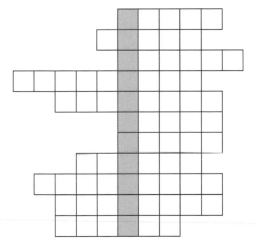

1) Put your hand over your mouth when you do this
2) Giggle
3) Animals drink from this
4) The study of places
5) Using the body
6) Chewy meat can be described as this
7) Not smooth
8) Plenty
9) Use this to talk to friends
10) Twenty six letters
11) The shape of a tennis ball

Now write the new word you will have made by reading the shaded column from top to bottom.

12) A disaster: _____

2 Write the missing words in these sentences.

She drew a _____ in her maths lesson.

In his English lesson he wrote a _____ of a famous person.

She took a lovely _____ with her new camera.

The actor signed his name in many _____ books.

Flowers had been planted in a _____ in the garden.

The joke made me _____ a lot.

The doctor gave her some medicine to help clear up her bad _____.

Words beginning with **im** or **in**

1 Focus on words

- Photocopy this page and the accompanying student worksheet. Discuss the focus words at the bottom of the page with the students. Ask them to write the words in the blank grid on their worksheet. You could dictate the words or, if appropriate, students could copy them from the set below.

- The completed grid on the worksheet, or the one below, could be laminated as a pocket reference card that students could refer to later.

- Discuss the fact that in most of the words **im** or **in** are prefixes that change the meanings of existing words to their opposites. You could ask the students to sort the words into two lists: words that begin with **im** and words that begin with **in**. Point out that some of the words cannot be made into meaningful related words if the **im** or **in** are removed e.g. *impaired* or *insurance*

- To analyse the words further, and if appropriate for your students, you could complete the following activities.

  Segmenting the words into their phonemes
  Explain to the students that they are going to segment some of the words into their separate sounds. Demonstrate with the word *impossible* by drawing lines between the graphemes that represent the separate phonemes: /i/m/p/o/ss/i/b/le/. In examining the words students may come up with different answers from each other but the important part of the activity is the process of listening to the sounds and observing how they are represented by graphemes.

  Splitting the words into their syllables (syllabification)
  For most students syllabification is much easier than segmenting. Explain that they are now going to split the words into 'chunks' of sound and give the example of *incredible: \in\cred\i\ble*. Can the students hear that the word can be split into four syllables?

2 Words in context

- When the students are ready ask them to complete the second activity on the worksheet, in one of two ways. They can either attempt to read the sentences themselves and write the missing words or they can listen to you dictating the sentences and write the missing words as you dictate them.

impossible	impatient	impressed	immature
impaired	impractical	impolite	imperfect
inactive	instant	influence	interest
incredible	insurance	independent	include
immodest	immobile	inexperienced	inedible

Words beginning with **im** or **in**

Name _____

1 Write the focus words in the spaces on this grid.

Choose words from the grid to complete the crossword.

Clues Across

2) Amazing
4) Unable to be done
5) Immediate
7) Babyish
10) Able to care for oneself
11) Not good at practical tasks

Clues Down

1) A hobby could be called this
3) Rude
4) A type of financial protection
6) Not perfect
8) Damaged
9) Still

2 Write the missing words in these sentences.

He wanted to _____ all the best players in the team.

Good teachers can have a positive _____ on their students.

The magician disappeared in an _____ .

It is important to have car _____ in case of an accident.

The night sky full of stars is an _____ sight.

It is _____ for humans to live without water.

The teacher was very _____ with the high standard of her pupils' spellings.

He had a lifelong _____ in archaeology.

Words beginning with up

1 Focus on words

- Photocopy this page and the accompanying student worksheet. Discuss the focus words at the bottom of the page with the students. Ask them to write the words in the blank grid on their worksheet. You could dictate the words or, if appropriate, students could copy them from the set below.

- The completed grid on the worksheet, or the one below, could be laminated as a pocket reference card that students could refer to later.

- Discuss some of the words in more detail e.g. the words *uplighter* and *downlighter* cannot be found in most dictionaries as they are newly invented words! Ask the students how many of them have *downlighters* in their kitchens or bathrooms. This helps students to appreciate that language is constantly evolving and new words are developed.

- To analyse the words further, and if appropriate for your students, you could complete the following activities.

  Segmenting the words into their phonemes
  Explain to the students that they are going to segment some of the words into their separate sounds. Demonstrate with the word *update* by drawing lines between the graphemes that represent the separate phonemes: */u/p/d/a/te/.* In examining the words students may come up with different answers from each other but the important part of the activity is the process of listening to the sounds and observing how they are represented by graphemes.

  Splitting the words into their syllables (syllabification)
  For most students syllabification is much easier than segmenting. Explain that they are now going to split the words into 'chunks' of sound and give the example of *upholstery: \up\hol\ste\ry\.* Can the students hear that the word can be split into four syllables?

2 Words in context

- When the students are ready ask them to complete the second activity on the worksheet.

upbeat	upbringing	update	upgrade
upheaval	uphold	upholstery	upkeep
uplighter	upload	upright	uprising
uproar	uproot	upset	upside
upstairs	upstream	uptight	upwards

Words beginning with up

Name _____

1 Write the focus words in the spaces on this grid.

Each of the focus words is a compound word made from the word **up** together with another word. In some of them we could replace **up** with **down** and make a new compound word.

Look again at each of the words below. If you can make a new word starting with **down** write your new word on the line. If you cannot make a new word, draw a cross on the line.

upbeat	_____	upright	_____
upbringing	_____	uprising	_____
update	_____	uproar	_____
upgrade	_____	uproot	_____
upheaval	_____	upset	_____
uphold	_____	upside	_____
upholstery	_____	upstairs	_____
upkeep	_____	upstream	_____
uplighter	_____	uptight	_____
upload	_____	upwards	_____

2 Try to write a sentence that contains an **up** word and a **down** word.

_____

_____

Position words

1 Focus on words

- Photocopy this page and the accompanying student worksheet. Discuss the focus words at the bottom of the page with the students. Ask them to write the words in the blank grid on their worksheet. You could dictate the words or, if appropriate, students could copy them from the set below.

- The completed grid on the worksheet, or the one below, could be laminated as a pocket reference card that students could refer to later.

- Most of the focus words are high frequency words and many of them are frequently misspelled. Some of them have appeared on previous worksheets in this book and can be revised; others have not been covered previously. Encourage the students to compare *door* with *corridor*. Extend the work by asking them to spell *indoors, outdoors, doorway, doorbell, doorknob, doormat, doorpost and doorstep*. Look carefully at the word *building* and extend the work by asking the students to spell *built, builder* and *building society*!

- To analyse the words further, and if appropriate for your students, you could complete the following activities.

  Segmenting the words into their phonemes
  Explain to the students that they are going to segment some of the words into their separate sounds. Demonstrate with the word *along* by drawing lines between the graphemes that represent the separate phonemes: /a/l/o/ng/. Now look at *building*: /b/ui/l/d/i/ng/. In examining the words students may come up with different answers from each other but the important part of the activity is the process of listening to the sounds and observing how they are represented by graphemes.

  Splitting the words into their syllables (syllabification)
  For most students syllabification is much easier than segmenting. Explain that they are now going to split the words into 'chunks' of sound and give the example of *between*: \be\tween\. Can the students hear that the word can be split into two syllables?

2 Words in context

- When the students are ready ask them to complete the second activity on the worksheet, which encourages them to write creatively, making use of as many of the focus words as possible.

above	across	along	around
below	between	high	inside
outside	through	under	upon
near	where	world	earth
window	door	corridor	building

Position words

Name _____

1 Write the focus words in the spaces on this grid.

2 Write a set of directions from where you are now to anywhere you like in the world! You must write in proper sentences and you must try to use as many of the position words as you can. Can you use all twenty?

_____

_____

_____

_____

_____

_____

_____

_____

_____

_____

_____

_____

_____

_____

_____

Alphabet speed sheet

Name _____

Sometimes you will need to use a dictionary to look up the spellings of words. You need to know your alphabet really well. Here is a fun activity for speeding up your alphabet skills.

Join the letters in alphabetical order as fast as you can. Time yourself.

This activity can be great fun when used in the form of a friendly competition. Students can all start at the same time and try to win the 'race' to complete the task. Alternatively, a student could complete the task on two or three occasions trying to beat her/his personal time.

Andrew Brodie: Supporting Spelling 11–12 © A & C Black 200